Seven Days in Paris

By Preston Brady III

A brief narrative with photos, but not a guidebook, based on a one week visit to Paris in November 2023. Suggestions for trip preparation and navigating and enjoying Paris during your stay for the 2024 Paris Summer Olympics and other first-time visits to this amazing city

Seven Days in Paris

by Preston Brady III © 2023   *100% Human Composed*

If you are a first-time visitor to Paris, this story is written for you. Although no stranger to international travel, November 2023 was my first visit to Paris. Alongside a monetary motivation, I was moved to write this because of how strongly I feel about the differences between all that I read and heard about Paris before my trip, and what I actually found: two very contrasting divisions.

In the interest of being timely I also believe some people could benefit from a fresh narrative about a Paris visit prior to the upcoming Paris Summer Olympics in 2024.

This is not a guidebook with train schedules and links to restaurant reservations. There are plenty of excellent guidebooks, with Lonely Planet standing out as one I have used for decades. This is my first-hand experience of what I found in Paris, with suggestions on how to make the most of your journey - to keep it as efficient, enjoyable and safe as possible. I share some of the restaurants and sites I visited, and make suggestions for metro travel, and things to consider before you book accommodations. More than anything though, I share my delightful surprise and just how much I loved the people of Paris - not that I did not expect to, but that they went against a common grain, against a stereotype floating around for decades. If you are visiting Paris for the first time you are indeed fortunate. What you will find will blow away any brain clutter you may have accumulated from social media, chat boards, old newspaper articles and even perhaps the experience of a few others who may have not been able to connect with Parisians in a way that we all should.

The best way for me to begin is to say Paris was everything I expected it to be, and so much that I did not expect it to be. As the Japanese are fond of saying: *genchi genbutsu* - go and see for yourself. *More than any other city, Paris is what you make it to be, what you yearn it to be.* What this means in terms of traveling there for the first time and seeking information about how to navigate and what to do, is take for a grain of salt most of the stereotypes you've heard and be prepared for something completely different, something far better.

It's a given that each person has their own experience but the biggest myth-buster I experienced during this trip was concerning the Parisians themselves. I was actually prepared generally for people who are not very helpful or too busy to be concerned about the trillionth tourist to visit their world famous city. I almost expected my head to be bitten off if I did not, in some instances, speak perfect French or to be shunned as yet another stupid American checking off another destination on their bucket list. In my worst-case imaginings I expected to be totally dependent on electronic language translators, to be navigating in a city so classy it did not have the time of day for some old guy from Alabama who mispronounces Marais and can't count past 5 in French. I kept telling my nephew the French don't pronounce the second part of a word. Give the second syllable an almost indecipherable "sa-wa" sound and you might be right.

I was relieved at how many of the myths that I had heard about Paris over the years, over the decades, turned out in my experience not to be true. I traveled with my nephew in early November 2023, and not once during our 7 day stay in Paris did we encounter a rude Parisian. In fact, several times Parisians stopped us and offered to assist as we discussed questions about which train to take and where to go. *Merci Beaucoup* to the woman walking her dog, who outside the Montparnasse–Bienvenüe metro station stopped and offered directions when she saw we were trying to determine the right direction to our hotel. Yes, we had electronic navigation applications and would have found our direction in a few minutes, but it was the thought and consideration of this Parisian stranger that made a difference. And the young woman who was passing us down in the same station as we huddled over a metro line map and plotted our journey from the 7th arrondissement to the 20th. She stopped unsolicited in her busy day and asked if she could assist. She confirmed our transfer station and metro line in about 10 seconds and was back on her way. These two unsolicited, helpful encounters mean a lot to a visitor and stand out as rebuttals to any contrary cliches about Parisians. At restaurants, museums, on the street everywhere we never once encountered a person who was unhelpful or uncaring. This is not to say they do not exist - they exist in every city in the world. It's just that we did not have any such negative encounters. Most spoke to us in English and we replied and spoke with limited French to show that we can try, and we do care about the language of the country we are visiting. On that point I believe it was helpful for us that we did show respect and effort for using simple and common French phrases, and I suppose perhaps someone who only speaks English and does not attempt to use any simple French phrases may encounter some resistance or even perhaps frustration on the part of the Parisian. I'm not sure, but we definitely were of the mindset that we wanted to attempt even if we mispronounced sometimes, to show respect and appreciation for the French language since we were in their country, in France. On the subject of language I would recommend knowing a few phrases and most definitely at least using phrases such as *bonjour, bonsoir, merci, merci beaucoup; pardonne moi.* If you are preparing several months or longer for your trip to Paris, fit a weekly immersion into French words and phrases into your routine, to make your journey even more enjoyable and successful. I am here to tell you that the French will not maliciously laugh at mispronunciations, but will laugh with joy that you are trying, and they will correct your faux paus free of charge. What better way to polish your French than in Paris?

Parisians have the most phenomenal sense of humor and we spoke to them in English and joked with them - they got it right away and played along. In some way most Parisians must be masters of sociology given the fact so many millions of people from around the world visit their city and over the years the Parisians get to know some of these people and get to know their habits and customs and so forth. They are the most keen observers and you may find them studying you on a train or in a restaurant. Don't be offended - it's their nature and they mean no harm.

Another myth that was dispelled was how to dress in Paris. Unless you're a fashion model, going to a four star Michelin restaurant for dinner, or attending some other formal event, you can dress just like most people in the world do on a daily basis.. Many Parisians wear blue jeans and logo style clothing - they dress most of them pretty casually. I laugh because I had read a few reviews online where it was strongly recommended that men wear black or brown leather shoes, but everywhere I saw tennis shoes and that's what I wore and nobody stared at my feet even as my shoes were a bright orange. Parisians dress just like most Americans, Americans dress just like Parisians. Now, in the summer if an American tourist is wearing colorful Bermuda shorts and a loud Hawaiian shirt and flip flops in central Paris, one may not find a single Parisian in that clothing. You will definitely be labeled American. Someone might even snicker. I saw another article online just this morning with a headline explaining how Parisians are able to spot American tourists by the way they dress. I did not read the article because, from experience, I don't think most Americans who visit Paris dress any differently than most Parisians or most anyone else in Europe or Asia. It seems like the whole world wears jeans, so how can you go wrong? I also doubt any more than a handful of Parisians spend time trying to discern American tourists from anyone else. They have far more important things to do.

Nothing I read prior to my trip prepared me for understanding Paris time. By Paris time I mean navigating, scheduling your day as a typical Parisian would do. Of course, Paris was 7 hours ahead of our time zone in Alabama. We did not experience any jet lag issues, perhaps because we arrived in the morning and stayed up until our normal bedtime. Even though our official hotel check-in time was supposed to be 3:00 PM, we appeared at the front desk around 12:30 PM and were checked in early without requesting it and with no questions asked. This may not be the case during the Olympics but we appreciated the early access to our room after the long flight.

Since we chose to stay in a more local neighborhood there were not as many recommendations for restaurants as you find in areas such as St. Germain du Pres, the Latin Quarter or the upper scale areas of the Right Bank near the Champs-Élysées. So we scouted on our own. One of our strategies was to scope restaurants and try to determine popularity based on whether the restaurant was busy. One problem was we were scoping too early and soon discovered many of the restaurants were closed at 6:00 PM, around the time we were scoping.

Many of the restaurants close after lunch and open again at 7:00 PM. We were told by a local resident that even 7:00 PM is considered too early for dinner in Paris. By around 7:00 to 8:00 PM we were able to see which restaurants were attracting local "regulars." We found a number of similarities in the restaurants that turned out to have what we found to be the best food and service. The best dinner restaurants were for the most part, but not in all cases, smaller, more intimate. Most of them had white table cloths. Most had professionally dressed waiters - dark slacks, white shirts, black shoes. Most had a host or hostess who greeted you as you walked in. We found that other restaurants that did not meet the above physical descriptions had waiters or hosts who came outside as you passed or if you stopped to view the glass-encased menu on the sidewalk in front of the restaurant. We reasoned they might be anxious for business and we pondered any reasons why this might be the case. Perhaps we were being too picky, but if the glass-enshrined menu case was dirty, we took this to mean perhaps the inside - especially what we could not see - might be unclean as well. If I had my way I would immediately receive a tour of the kitchen of each restaurant I visit anywhere in the world, including America, but unfortunately I don't think most proprietors would agree to such a request. However, a quick visit to the bathroom might shed light on the overall sanitation of a restaurant. To be clear, out of the dozens of restaurants we visited we really only encountered one that displayed bad hygiene and that was in the basement bathroom. We noticed that it was common to find the bathrooms were logically located in the basements of many restaurants, and the storage rooms were often in adjacent areas. It should be no surprise there are apps one can use to gauge the hygiene of Parisian restaurants, which include Paris health inspection reports that rate a large number of restaurants including flagging any that need immediate correction. We were not aware of the apps prior to our visit, and I am not sure we would have used one, but they are available for people who may want that extra layer of confidence in an eating establishment.

Many of the exceptional dinner restaurants had chalk board menus, sometimes to supplement a paper menu and sometimes only the daily chalkboard display. We found the chalkboard menus to be more desirable because it appeared the daily menu was fashioned around the fresh ingredients and fresh seafood and other entrees they were able to procure that day. A yellow flag for me is a plastic menu that is six pages of dozens and dozens of food items. This tells me there has to be a good mix of processed or frozen food on the menu, because a chef is not going to be able to procure that large amount of fresh ingredients on a daily or likely even a weekly basis. We did encounter at least one such restaurant and politely left before we ordered. The food would have probably been acceptable but definitely not exceptional. Around 5:30 PM we noticed the sidewalk sections of a number of restaurants were bustling with activity. But as we scoped the tables for food we found instead bottles of beer and glasses of wine. These were Parisians who gathered together after work for a drink or two. The blank faces of commuters on the streets transformed into jovial animation as I wished I could be a French speaking fly on those walls as they all chatted and enjoyed the best time of the day - being off work.

Most of these menus were of course in French and some of the items we could translate because many French words are similar to English. Whatever we could not translate, the waiters were always happy to explain, sometimes in broken English but the effort was definitely greatly appreciated. And sometimes you just feel Googled and Binged out, right? Some menus translated items into English underneath the French version. To give an idea of what language limitations can do, in one breakfast restaurant the menu said three fried eggs. I asked the waiter for only one fried egg and was served four fried eggs. We were having a late breakfast and unfortunately for us the staff chose that time to sweep the floor, clean the place, even if they did not seem to notice a few spider webs on the ceiling in the dining area. I suppose this could have been our punishment for sleeping in and trying to have a late breakfast. My travel companion was in search of real eggs - the ones that have a brilliant yellow, almost orange yolk. These are usually organic, cage-free, farm hatched eggs, as opposed to mass produced, non-organic, or even fake eggs. Apparently fake eggs may actually be a thing but that will have to be the subject of another book. One other thing, in some restaurants a request for bacon may result in receiving ham. We did not see this type of confusion in the better restaurants we visited. I tell you all this to try and help you avoid bad, wasted money dining experiences. Paris has about 44,000 restaurants and while it is one of the culinary capitals of the world, anyone with enough money can open a restaurant, but that does not always make it a great or even good restaurant. However, I have never been anywhere with so many great restaurants. With a little extra effort visitors should be able to end up in mostly superb restaurants, of which are everywhere.

The best lunch and dinner restaurants all brought hors d'oeuvres immediately to the table, in the form of green and black olives and sometimes bite-sized French bread toast with a sprinkling of fresh vegetables and herbs. A few not-so-great restaurants we mistakenly patronized brought water and usually a basket of bread. Bread is like air in Paris: it is everywhere and usually fresh and delicious. We sometimes drank the tap water and had no issues. Bottled water in restaurants is not cheap, but in local grocery stores you can purchase 6 and 12 packs for around 4 euro. In the little convenience stores a 12 ounce bottle is about 1 euro. If you are outlining your budget in Paris and you drink a fair amount of bottled water, include water as a line item.

Suffice it to say *that in the very touristy areas a very busy restaurant does not necessarily translate to a great restaurant.* Near the Museum of Natural History there was one such crowded restaurant. It was large and bustling with tourists during a recent lunch hour. The quiche Lorraine was not very good, was too large, had too many processed-looking little square bites of ham, was not creamy at all, and did not appear to be or taste like it was made on premises. I imagined it was delivered in a large box along with dozens of other frozen quiche. If a restaurant portion is extremely large I start to suspect perhaps they are trying to impress the diner with size so perhaps one will overlook quality. In my experience when an entree is superb, there won't be enough of it to go around. A chef spends a great deal of time preparing a choice entree, and a slice of quiche the size of Manhattan is probably not the result of a unique culinary effort but rather a mass produced product in a factory somewhere. I admit there could be exceptions or I might altogether be wrong, but I can only go by my experience and gut, and my gut told me that slice of quiche was a plain tasting concoction of powdered eggs, processed cheese and factory chopped squares of ham. I ate a few bites just for show and chalked the whole experience off as you are never too old to learn something new about restaurants.

A garden salad came already with a mayonnaise style dressing mixed in, which a companion diner did not appreciate. We joked the rest of the trip that we must make it a point to go back to that restaurant! Rest assured we did not. We surmised the restaurant was crowded because people wanted to sit down after so much touring and at that point they were not particularly caring of the quality of food, especially for lunch. It was a clean, smartly designed restaurant serving processed, frozen food.

My travel companion was on a mission to find an Italian restaurant serving brick-oven cooked pizza. On another day we spontaneously wandered into a restaurant to try the pizza. Read: not always a smart thing to do. A companion found the bathroom area to be very unsanitary and the Margherita pizza (you see this pizza on a lot of menus) was plain, bland and we only ate a few bites before the companion had visited the restroom. We did not complain, we just paid the bill and left. It did not make sense to engage in any negativity in a restaurant we knew we would never again visit. We weren't angry, just disappointed.

We very quickly learned how to spot good restaurants and the above two examples were really our only undelightful dining experiences.

If you are in Montparnasse, 7th arrondissement, an exceptional restaurant specializing in seafood is *Le Bistro du Dôme, 1 Rue Delambre, 75014.* Both the sebring and grouper fish were excellent. If they happen to have the fig dessert on the menu it's the one to choose as it turned out to be the very best dessert I had in Paris.

Le Bistro du Dôme, 1 Rue Delambre, 75014, Paris, 2023 Preston Brady III

We ate twice at *Auberge de Venise, 10 Rue Delambre*, having steak the first night and lasagne the second. Both excellent food and service. During our second visit we sat next to an American couple who said they had been coming to the Italian restaurant for 25 years. The woman was from Oklohama and once lived in Paris and played the organ at the Cathedral of Notre Dame. Perhaps the excellent glass of red wine catapulted our excitement at meeting someone who actually played the pipe organ at the most famous cathedral in the world. The gentleman was from New York. We assume they met in Paris many years ago and fell in love. We enjoyed their company.

If you are staying in Montparnasse and want a full, American style breakfast you only have to get on the nearby metro and exit at the St-Germain-des-Prés stop. As soon as you emerge from the underground metro you will see the restaurant Les Deux Magots (Translates to *Two Chinese figurines* because this used to be a novelty shop. The two statues are still on the premises.) Of course this cafe is famous as a favorite of Hemingway, Picasso, Joyce, Sartre and Breton to name a few. We only waited for a few minutes to be seated inside. The service and food were superb. If that is not enough literary prowess to make you light-headed, the very famous Café de Flore is practically next door. While we only had champagne and coffee at this cafe, another diner attested to the excellence of the French onion soup. I am not sure one can visit Paris without tasting the French onion soup in at least one restaurant. We had a full breakfast at Les Deux Magots to include sunny-side up eggs, bacon, fresh fruit, freshly squeezed orange juice, and French bread with jam.

Something you might not give much thought but perhaps should, is the exact name of the restaurant you wish to visit, and close attention to restaurant signage. If a restaurant is situated near a metro stop or landmark, it may include in its name the landmark location. For example, near Pere Lachaise cemetery one will find several establishments with Pere Lachaise in their name. You may be looking for Pere Lachaise Cafe when you instead find Pere Lachaise Brasserie or Pere Lachaise Restaurant. This is not to say any one restaurant is better than the other, but you could be meeting someone or you have your appetite set on a particular restaurant you have researched prior to your trip. Brightly-lit signage and multiple signs on one restaurant could merit a second look before you commit to dining.

After breakfast you can stroll the famous streets of St-Germain-des-Prés, lined with pastry and cheese shops, clothing stores and more. We found some nice souvenirs in this location, including pairs of very thick, wooly socks with the word Paris knitted in. Speaking of souvenirs, once you are in the most popular tourist areas such as the Louvre and Eiffel Tower there are a small number of street vendors who sell trinkets easy to pack and carry back home. I purchased several miniature Eiffel towers for one euro each. I am not sure if this was just luck on our part but it was noticed that street vendors do not approach you to buy their wares. Perhaps this is a law in Paris, but unlike several other countries I have visited, this agreement, if you will, was appreciated.

Speaking of souvenirs, many people wait until their last few days to try and make those last minute purchases. From experience I recommend starting early in your visit so you do not have to feel rushed during the last part of your visit, when you may already be a bit on the tired side and can use any additional relaxation. Also, consider buying French cheese to take home to family and friends. A cheese shop we visited near our hotel recommended the type of cheese we preferred: (nothing closely resembling Limburger) packaged it for travel including a heavy shrink-wrap so we could pack it in our carry-on bag for the flight home. My only regret is that I did not buy more cheese. The shop is Fromagerie Beillevaire Paris Delambre, 8 Rue Delambre, 75014. It's currently closed on Mondays and closes during certain parts of the day so check online first before making a special visit to this perfect fromagerie. There are excellent cheese shops throughout Paris and I recommend you find a few minutes to partake during your visit.

I am fairly certain French authorities will not allow visitors to leave Paris who have not indulged in one of the national desserts, the macaron. You will see them everywhere in the hundreds of bakeries, and the flavors hazelnut and pistachio are popular and often served with a similar flavored gelato. These will also make an excellent gift to bring home to a friend. If you are on a diet you will need to temporarily suspend it while in Paris. No one should be deprived of the other worldly culinary treats of Paris, France.

Most people carry a small backpack or shoulder bag of some type as they are touring Paris. We were recommended to keep it close at hand and take extra caution in crowded areas. This may be more of a concern during the very busy seasons when people may bump into one another. We rarely had that much of a crowded experience, but I can imagine, for example during the Summer Olympics in 2024 this will occur. In these cases one can maneuver their bag to the front of the body and take extra precautions. We read there are professional teams of pick-pockets and apparently they may use clever schemes working together to cause distraction enough to possibly complete a theft. Fortunately we did not have such encounters. I would say it is accurate that it would be the exception, not the rule, that anyone would approach you as if to ask a question. We only had it once and it was someone in front of a building carrying a clipboard. She probably wanted us to sign a petition or perhaps to sell us something but as she spoke French and we did not understand her we politely kept moving along. People mostly kept to themselves but we did have several people stop and offer us assistance to board a train or find a museum. On this note we found Parisians polite and helpful in many instances.

We chose to stay at the Hotel Lenox Montparnasse, 15 Rue Delambre. 75014.

Hotel Lenox, Montparnasse, Paris - Preston Brady III 2023

Notice the street address is very similar to two of the restaurants I mentioned earlier. We literally walked out the door of the hotel to find the Italian and fish restaurants. This 3 star hotel was recommended online and we agree it is a good place to stay. Of course, like many Paris hotels the room was *very* small. I believe they have larger, penthouse style rooms on the top, 6th floor. We stayed on the 4th floor, overlooking Rue Delambre Street. The hotel is very quiet except on some mornings the garbage trucks or course make noise. I got used to it and dozed back to sleep. I informed my travel companion that it could be worse: we could be staying in a hotel in a popular night district and be subjected to the abundant camaraderie of younger people who relish in the good chaos of inebriated singing in the streets and boisterous celebration of life in the wee hours of the morning before the bars close. Most bars close by 2:00 AM but there are some that encourage acceleration of joie de vivre until 6:00 AM. I have read stories in which some hotel stays included this unexpected, unwanted very late-night distraction, so prior to making reservations perhaps have direct contact with hotel staff or even view in a maps application the proximity of the hotel to any possible bars, pubs or late night venues. If the hotel is adequately soundproofed and you are staying in a room on a very upper floor, noise on the street may not be a concern. If you are one of those who want to be part of this all night experience in the City of Light after dark, then by all means book a nearby hotel. On a positive note you will only have a few steps to stumble joyfully back to your room and sleep until noon if you so please. Drink plenty of water and don't forget the aspirin.

In our hotel room there was a little balcony that opened to the street. The room was climate-controlled but as it was cool most of the time during our stay, we did not need to use heat or air. There was a controller on a wall, set to 20 degrees Celsisus. I believe the system automatically turned on a few times. The hotel offered one double bed or two twin beds and we reserved two twin beds. As the two beds are butted up against one another (and there is no space to move them) I am not sure paying the extra 20 euro a night was worth this, but each having our own set of blankets probably made it more comfortable as we did not have to compete for the covers and changing sleep positions was possible without disturbing the other. My travel companion accused me of snoring one night but I know this can't be true. I have never been accused of snoring and I won't take that kind of accusation.

Twin bed room, Hotel Lenox Montparnasse, Paris 2023, Preston Brady III

The bathroom was very nice with a modern shower and toilet. Everything worked right and there was no shortage of hot water. Near the door was a small closet for hanging and storing clothing, a small refrigerator and a small coffee or tea service. There was shampoo and body wash provided as well as a hair dryer. You may need to bring any additional toiletries you require. If for some reason you are communicating with the hotel on another matter, you might ask which toiletries and extras are included in the room. If you are like me, you want to minimize what you pack for your trip. If you use certain products due to skin sensitivity or allergies then of course you may need to bring your own. Be sure to check the airline dry and liquid package limitations.

There was an extra bolt lock on the room door, which we used but we felt safe in the hotel. The hotel itself was very quiet at night. Of course I cannot speak of any possible noise levels at different times of the year, but our experience was peaceful. If you are coming from America you will need a small electrical wall converter if you need to charge anything such as a phone. I purchased one online before the trip. Paris is on 220-Volt while America is on 110-120 V.

Hotel Lenox offers breakfast at an additional charge, which we chose not to reserve because our idea was to stroll the streets for the wonderful pastries offered by the numerous bakeries. Access to the breakfast buffet which serves until 11:00 AM is an additional 19 euro if you choose to indulge on any one day. Coffee and tea are free. We did have breakfast in the hotel one morning and it featured scrambled eggs, bacon, ham and sausage, cereals, pastries, croissants, fresh fruit, fresh juices. If you are going to have a busy day, having breakfast at the hotel will save time. There is also a bar that is unmanned and uses the honor system by completing a brief form as to what you poured or took from the refrigerator. A cold beer or glass of champagne was 7 Euros. Since there are a few convenience stores close by, if one wants a nightcap drink or some bottled water before bed, you can simply buy it and bring it to your room at a lower cost. It's best to pay with euros because these local stores often include an international transfer fee of as much as 2 euros if you pay the debit method. Check your bank statements each morning for any anomalies.

The one elevator in the hotel is very small and will fit no more than 4 people or 250 kilograms/552 pounds- and that is a tight squeeze. We did find that during morning hours the maid staff made active use of the elevator to travel up and then down to the basement where linens and supplies are stored. Sometimes it's best to walk down the stairs if you have an appointment to keep. If you are in a hotel with multiple upper floors, and it's not a major chain hotel, you may want to check on the number of elevators. During the Olympics you could find yourself waiting on the elevator for what you consider an inordinate amount of time.

In Paris most hotels request that you leave your door key at the front desk each time you leave. We never had a problem or delay in retrieving the key once back from an excursion. I have read comments online where some travelers are very attached to their room keys and do not like the idea of parting with it. Our hotel staff said it was not required but they preferred it. We complied with their wishes and never had to wait more than a minute for the key. The bed and bath linens were freshly changed every day without fail. They always waited until we left the room, and never asked to enter while we were still in the room. The front desk staff were always helpful and understanding. In the dining room the service staff member may ask for your room number while you are pouring coffee. If you did not prepay for breakfast and are not having the hotel breakfast that morning, inform the staff person you are having coffee or tea only so your room is not charged for breakfast. Ask for a review of your bill when you check-out. We had no invalid room charges on our final bill.

On the note of a climate controlled room, since many visitors will be in Paris during the summer I advise confirming with your hotel, Vrbo or Airbnb before booking, whether or not the air-conditioning is in *good* working order. I suggest asking in French and English, and your native language if not English. You may even want to reconfirm a few days before departure because it can be very unpleasant to have to sleep in a hot room after you have been outside and active most of the day. I did try to reserve a flat via Vrbo that featured a nice view of the Eiffel Tower, but did not receive a response from the owner in the 24 hour deadline mandated by Vrbo. The cost was going to be about 325 per night for this rooftop apartment. Honestly, there were a lot of variables that I felt may have gone unanswered and might leave some important details to chance - which isn't always a bad thing, but I took the no response from the owner as a sign that perhaps there were some issues of concern or perhaps the apartment was already booked even though it did not appear to be when I requested the reservation. I have used both Vrbo and Airbnb on other international vacations and they have always been a fairly good experience. If you are considering these non-hotel options during the Paris Summer Olympics make sure you do all of your homework and feel totally confident in your selection and security of your reservation, i.e., it will be empty and clean, waiting for your arrival. While not all reviews are fair and accurate, for the most part one can ascertain a very good idea of what to expect, and to confirm with the owner any corrections or suggestions made by previous travelers. But at the end of the day a hotel reservation almost 100% of the time guarantees a room will be waiting for you after your long flight to Paris. If there is, prior to the trip, excellent rapport with the landlord of a studio apartment or flat, this may be a better option than a hotel by having more room and perhaps your own place without some of the delays experienced at a hotel. Weigh all options carefully.

By the way, for all the media attention to a supposed bedbug epidemic in Paris, the subject was not mentioned once in Paris and we never saw or felt any bedbugs. It almost caused me to believe in conspiracy theories (except I do believe the world is round, not flat) although I assume there had been some sort of issue with the bugs in Paris somewhere, sometime, but then again it could have been all made up. I felt sort of deprived that I could not come back home and say I was in Paris during the infamous 2023 Bedbug Epidemic.

I definitely recommend having some euro in your pocket, as many of the stores charge an international transaction fee if you use a debit card. The charge was about 2 euro - too much in my opinion. At the start of Rue Delambre is a bank with two outside ATM machines which I used several times and had no issues. The ATM menu offered a choice of withdrawing "with conversion" or "without conversion." When the transaction failed after selecting "with conversion" I chose "without conversion" and received the requested funds. The defaults are up to 90 euro or you can select to enter a larger amount if you want. Some of the less popular establishments did not accept American Express , but almost all well-known, popular restaurants accepted the card. If you are using credit cards I recommend having at least two of the major carriers, such as American Express, Mastercard or Visa.

As you stroll the beautiful streets of Paris, especially in local neighborhoods and during morning and evening commute hours, be mindful of locals who are anxious to get to work on time or get home to enjoy their own dinner and evenings. We would move over to the right of the sidewalk to allow them to pass, since we were on vacation and not in any hurry. Showing this politeness will usually result in mutual politeness on their part.

Before departing from home it's best to reserve the Louvre and Eiffel Tower, both of which we visited and did not have long waits. For an additional $25.00 Euro per person one can shoot up to the very top of the Eiffel and receive a glass of champagne poured into a plastic cone-shaped container with the Eiffel tower imprinted, to be kept as a souvenir.

The Hooded Nephew, 300 meters high atop the Eiffel Tower, 2023, Preston Brady III

Even in early November the Louvre was fairly busy and the jostling around the Mona Lisa was like being at an in-person celebrity event. I can't help but wonder what De Vinci would think if he could somehow know the cult status of his Mona Lisa. Someone asked me what is the big deal about this nice but not necessarily extraordinary painting. It appears it was ahead of its time in the world of 16th century paintings in that it was a realistic portrait of the face of a real person. Consider the millions of similar paintings that followed and continue to be produced, by thousands of artists around the world. Many of them are even more beautiful and realistic than the Mona Lisa. The problem is they were not painted in 1503. Who said timing is everything? They were apparently right.

Jostling for a look at Mona Lisa at the Louvre, Paris 2023 Preston Brady III

I can imagine during the Olympics it will be much busier. Plan to spend at least a few hours if not more at the Louvre, just to see the famous De Vinci painting, in the Italian gallery deep inside the museum. Obviously there are many other famous paintings and sculptures at the Louvre, including The Raft of Medusa, (Théodore Géricault) The Wedding at Cana, (Veronese) and the iconic Venus de Milo marble statue.

The Eiffel Tower has one very large elevator to take you up and down the lower observation tower where outside on the day of our visit it was very windy. With the champagne bar ticket, a second line, smaller elevator, takes you to the very top. Both elevators have glass windows for viewing as you raise and lower inside the tower. Of course there is a souvenir shop and there is a line-style restaurant where you choose food and then find a place to sit. We did not indulge in the restaurant as it seemed a good place only if you were really hungry and needed some quick nourishment. I believe it was at the Dupleix metro station we found a small flea market of food, clothing and many other items, which closed at 2:00 PM. It would be an interesting side-visit if you are early to your Eiffel Tower visit, or perhaps afterwards.

We also enjoyed the National Museum of Natural History that has over 67 million specimens. Unfortunately, we were unable to take in all 67 million. We definitely saw relics of skeletons, body parts inside and out of humans and animals that we had never seen, including the innards of a large elephant, and replicas of tongues of various homo sapiens over time.

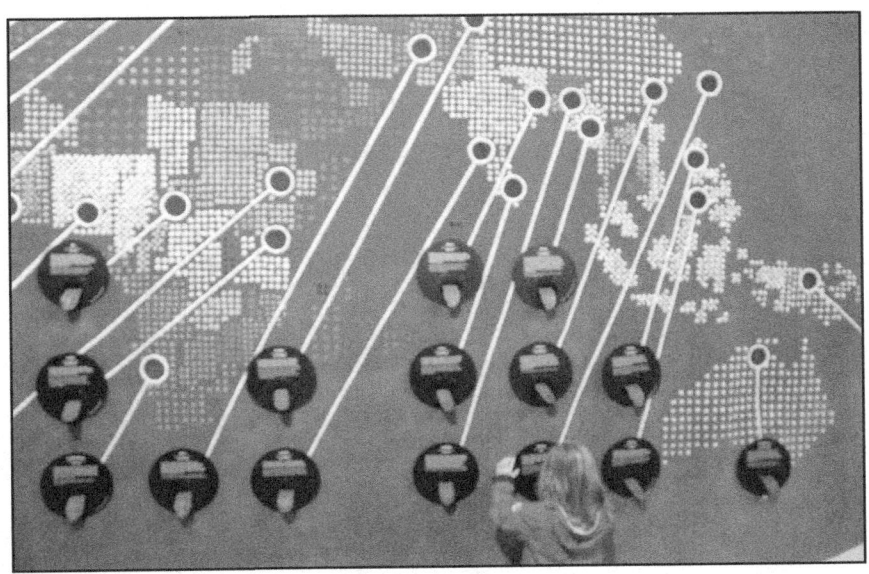

Tongues, Paris Museum of Natural History, Preston Brady III 2023

There were many interactive displays that seemed especially educational and delightful for children, and sometimes adults even commandeered the displays. Although we did not make a reservation for this museum, it is recommended during the Olympics should you want to find the time to visit.

We found a walk along the Champs-Élysées to be very nice, as it is billed in some descriptions as the most beautiful street in the world. Having read some of the history of this street it is known that King Louis XIV ordered what was then known as the Avenue des Tuileries to be widened, to give it more grandeur. Now it is home to many of the great fashion designers of the world. There were lines to enter some of these prestigious stores.

Louis Vuitton, Paris 2023 Preston Brady III

We strolled and came upon Hôtel Barrière Le Fouquet's Paris, 99 Avenue des Champs-Élysées. The restaurant immediately looked appealing for its fine decor and smartly dressed waiters. The obligatory white table cloths were in abundance. We had lunch at Fouquet's inside the hotel and my companion thoroughly enjoyed the lamb chops and I a bowl of perhaps the very best ever French onion soup.

French Onion Soup, Fouquet's , Preston Brady III 2023

We shared a raspberry and basil shortbread tart with sorbet and coulis, which like everything we had here was delicious.

In France they not only offer glasses of champagne, they often offer to elevate the experience with an added peach and Cointreau or Grand Marnier splash. At one bar they even mixed in Mescal with the peach liqueur and it made for perhaps the strongest glass of champagne in my life. At one restaurant the champagne even came with a sizzling sparkler, an only in Paris affair. I believe we were very fortunate to be able to stroll into Fouquet's for lunch without a reservation, so if you are visiting during the Summer Olympics perhaps make a reservation. Of course in this case we acted spontaneously, which added to our experience, but in a busy season or event it might be best to plan ahead so as to not be shut out of the best places to dine.

From Forquet's we made our way up the Avenue des Champs-Élysées to the Arc de Triomphe, a monument to those who perished during the French Revolution and Napoleonic War.

Arc de Triomphe, Paris, 2023 Preston Brady III - Zoom in to see the people on top of the Arc.

It was about a twenty minute walk from the restaurant, straight ahead. Once you approach the traffic turn-around in front of the monument, find the underground tunnels leading to the other side of the street on which the monument proudly stands. You do not want to try and cross the street in the heavy, circular traffic. Although web site venues mention an elevator inside the monument, we did not see any being used and were labeled for use by those physically challenged. We, like everyone else there climbed 284 narrow, spiral steps, plus an additional 46 once we reached what is called the attic room. There was a landing where some people rested at mid-climb (yes, I stopped.) It is quite a climb but at the top outside are splendid views of Paris. This visit cost 13 euros each and we felt it was a monument we should see in Paris. An eternal flame burns outside at ground-level. I will note we did not reserve or visit the Palace of Versaille, for personal reasons we wanted to spend more time among the locals in Montparnasse. However, if you want to visit this "must-see' palace I recommend dedicating a full day, especially during a busy season, as you must take a train to the location just outside Paris, wait in perhaps a line, or two, and then the grounds itself has more to see than possible even doing multiple visits. Because you should plan for unexpected delays, dedicating a full day to this adventure is probably the best choice. Some people rent the bicycles offered to tour the Versailles Park, but it is stated that bicycles are not allowed in the royal gardens of the palace and adjacent Trianon Gardens. The approximate cost to rent a bicycle in this venue is about 10 euro per hour or 21 euro for half a day. If you manage to accomplish this visit in less than a day, then you have unexpected leisure time to make an unplanned visit to perhaps another site near your accommodation in Paris. You will need to reserve and purchase tickets for Versaille prior to your departure from home. If you are already prepared for possible glitches and delays, then you won't be surprised and it won't be as disappointing. As you may have gathered, there is no lack of very historically significant places to visit.

If you wish to visit the Catacombs in the 14th arrondissement, where over 6 million people are interned and many openly in skeleton form inside the walls, it is imperative that you make a reservation. The site only allows about 200 people at one time, and thousands of people want to visit the catacombs on any given day. If you do take a chance, notice there is a sign near the line. If it says "sold out," then if you don't have a ticket you need to find somewhere else to visit. Please note and remember, most museums in Paris are closed on Mondays and Tuesdays. If you are making reservations online this should be apparent, but if you are making unplanned spontaneous visits to museums and national shrines, it's likely they will be closed on Mondays and Tuesdays.

As it turns out we found this out the hard way with a planned visit to the most famous cemetery in the world, Pere Lachaise, on the day before our last day in Paris, a Tuesday. I must not have thought of the cemetery as a "museum" but now we all know, it is. I am lucky to have a friend who lives in Paris, who agreed to meet us at a cafe near the cemetery in the 20th arrondissement. Since the cemetery was closed our friend took us by short train ride to a street in Montmartre lined with music stores mainly catering to guitar players. We saw a shop catering only to left-handed guitar players, and a shop where you could order a custom made guitar they assembled from various quality parts. There were shops that only sold guitar pedals or accessories, that only sold bass guitars or only ukuleles. I had never seen several streets of a neighborhood dedicated almost exclusively to musical instruments and accessories. We appreciated this off the beaten path surprise.

The Left-Handed Shop - Photo: Preston Brady III   2023

A short walk from here we found the artistic, inner neighborhood of Montmartre, beautifully lined with cafes, restaurants, bakeries, and a small town square where oil painters sold their works and others offered to sketch you. I found a very small painting of the neighborhood for 40 euros, something I could easily pack in my carry on bag. One got the sense of the old, artistic Paris here and although we could not navigate the entire neighborhood, it was great to get a taste of it.

It took some serious climbing of steps to reach another, nearby neighborhood, Marais, (pronounced *Ma-Ray*) but the view from the top was worth it. Even in November the area was teeming with tourists. These two neighborhoods can be visited in one afternoon but as this was our last full day in Paris our friend gave us the abbreviated tour because we still had to see the Cathedral of Notre Dame. Even though the cathedral is closed for renovations, its beauty and sheer power radiate from the exterior. Here along the right bank of the Seine river a tour boat happened by and the area is dotted as most of Paris with restaurants and cafes. In case you arrive in Paris prior to the Olympics and are there on July 14th, this is Bastille Day, a national holiday commemorating the French Revolution. It would probably be awesome to be able to ride in one of the tour boats along the Seine that night and observe the fireworks and celebrations.

The famous bookstore Shakespeare and Company is very near the Cathedral and we stopped and I purchased *Paris: The Biography of a City by Colin Jones*. I read almost half of this book on the way back home and look forward to reading the rest. It captured Paris from the first 100 years and forward. It would be an excellent book to read before your trip, to get a real sense of the history of this amazing city.

We stopped in a bar for a beer where the bartender told us the owner was from Louisiana and also owned another bar down the street. We requested to know the best restaurant in the area but a survey of what was recommended, from the exterior, did not capture our appetite. Which brings me to the subject of requesting recommendations from barkeeps and others who may recommend an establishment because it is part of their domain. That night we had our last Paris dinner on this trip at the Italian restaurant *Le Bistro du Dôme, 1 Rue Delambre, 75014,* making it the only restaurant we dined for dinner twice.

If you are a fan of steak and fries there is likely no better place than *Relais de l'Entrecôte*. There are three in Paris - one near our hotel at 101 Blvd Du Montparnasse 75006, one at 20 Rue Saint Benoit, 75006 in Saint-Germain-des-Pres and one, Marbeuf, near the Champs-Élysées at 15 Rue Marbeuf - 75008. This is a first-come first-served restaurant so reservations are not accepted.

We arrived at the restaurant in Montparnasse around 7:30 PM and it was full to capacity and the line outside turned out to be about 30 minutes long.

Relais de l'Entrecôte , Paris, Preston Brady III 2023

My nephew asked a woman in front of us why the restaurant was so popular and she replied "because it's good." My nephew thinks perhaps she was confused but I think she answered in a typical Parisian fashion. Perhaps she was an existentialist. Anyway, she was right. This restaurant offers no choices except whether you want your steak medium or well done - no medium well or other option, but you have a choice of beverages. A walnut salad is served with mustard vinaigrette and it was delicious and it's the only choice. You are served a generous helping of steak and homemade shoestring fries and once you finish you are offered another generous helping of each. The steak sauce recipe is apparently a secret but there are rumors the famous pea green colored sauce is made from tarragon and basil and a host of other secret ingredients. The beauty of the steak sauce is its profound subtleness. It's neither strong nor lacking in flavor. My guess is its brilliance is in so many ingredients that all come together with not one standing above the other - a very democratic flavor. We ordered a chocolate ice-cream dessert that had vanilla in its center and which was doused with rum at our table and **flambéed** right there. It was delicious. When we left around 10:00 PM the restaurant was still almost full but there was no line so diners could walk in and be immediately seated. In case you make it to Zurich or Geneva there is a restaurant in these two cities as well.

Relais de l'Entrecôte copy of original, handwritten menu, 2023 Preston Brady III

The metro lines seemed fairly easy to understand and navigate. Although there are over 300 metro stations, there are only 14 numbered lines and you will use only a few lines and stations to navigate the main parts of Paris. The display maps throughout the metro stations show the color-coded lines and explain any needed transfers by posting the train line numbers under the appropriate stations. There are two additional, newer lines named

3bis and 7bis from Château-Landon station to Gambetta station. The lines we used the most were lines 4, 6, 12 and 1. Trains run around 5:30 AM to 12:40 AM Sunday-Thursday, 5:30 AM-1:40 AM Fridays and Saturdays. The frequency depends on the time of day, meaning more trains will run during peak hours. I would be surprised if metro hours were not extended during the Olympics, or perhaps even operated around the clock. A word of caution - there are small gaps between the train doors and platforms at some stations and the automated train announcements often warn you of such. Also, you may notice not all train doors open at stops, but there are handles on the doors and I saw locals use these to open doors from outside and inside at some stops. I'm not sure this is standard or permitted but just in case, when the train is fully stopped a flip of the handle appears to open a closed door. Just pay attention to the color coded lines and follow those lines on the maps to your destination. Note, you may have to transfer at a station and the Montparnasse-Bienvenue is one such transfer point. Sometimes we asked the ticket attendant and they almost always provide the name of the station we either needed to transfer or to depart at for our destination. Having navigated with limited dexterity the rail systems of Tokyo, we found the Paris Metro to be refreshing.

There will be numerous Olympic events in other cities in France and the TGV train system is the best option for these high-speed rail journeys.

There are four train stations in Paris from which the TGV trains leave and arrive: Gare du Nord, Gare de Lyon, Gare de l'Est and Gare Montparnasse. There is also a terminal at Charles de Gaulle airport, on level 1 of terminal 2, under the Sheraton hotel. The terminals 2D/2F and 2C/2E provide access to the station which is level 4.

Using the Paris metro, the service attendants you will see at each entrance do not accept cash - they accept cards only. However, some stations accept euros at the ticket terminals. The basic tickets are one-way and most of the time would not be needed to exit. There are instances where in mid-journey while transferring trains, attendants may stand on the paths and verify tickets. So, keep your train tickets until you have made the exit to your destination. A better option may be to purchase a metro pass for your entire stay, which runs from about 42 to 72 euros for a 5 day stay for zones 1-5. There is a Navigo card that can be purchased at the airport and at train stations. It requires a photo at an additional charge and has some limitations such as if you arrive in Paris on a Friday you can't use the pass that weekend, but overall it appears to be a good value of about 30 euros and approximately twenty trips. The ticket kiosks at the train stations allow for translation into English and other languages. Even if you buy metro passes there may be times when you still have to buy a train ticket. Don't be disappointed. Expect the unexpected and plan to spend a little more during your stay than you had originally thought.

You can also download the free Paris Metro app called Next Stop Paris. I have not used this app but it appears it could be a very useful trip planner. You can also purchase your metro pass up to six days in advance of arriving. If you are traveling to Paris during the Olympics it would seem having a pass would be in your very best interest given the number of people who will be in the city and having the ability to avoid some lines such as the lines for purchasing tickets. Using the app will also save you from having to use the large metro train line wall maps, which are likely to have quite a few people hovering over them and could cause some delays in catching your trains.

A few train etiquette rules, most of which seem to be common sense: don't stand at a train door at which passengers will be exiting. Stand aside and allow them to exit before you enter the train. *But do note the doors seem to close rather quickly* so don't linger too far back or too long entering or exiting the train. If you get on a train but fellow companions fail to get on in time, text them and make an agreement at which train station to meet. If your destination stop is clear to all, then text to meet at that stop. If the destination/train stop was still unclear or in discussion then text *I am getting off at the next stop and will wait for you.* Just in case there is a delay in sending and receiving texts, which we did encounter once or twice, make a preset agreement on what to do if separated in a metro station. This is not a bad idea to use at all busy locations. A few times I had to scan the crowd for a few minutes at the Louvre to find a travel companion. Just say: if we get lost, meet inside at the front exit of the building. Texting usually works but as previously stated there is sometimes a long delay. You might be able to call your companions but sometimes there are country code issues. Don't depend totally on electronics. Pretend it's 40 years ago and plan what you will do in the event you get separated from travel companions.

There are some fold-up seats on the trains, meaning you flip them down to take a seat. If the train is very crowded most Parisians will not use these seats in order to allow for more passengers on the train to stand. On very full trains it is recommended not to use these small fold-down seats. Some Parisians may glare at you or even make a comment if you use the fold-down seats on a very crowded train. It goes without saying seats should be yielded to passengers who need them more than others.

Sometimes things happen on the train lines and there may be an announcement in French and perhaps - but not always - in other languages. In one instance a train we were on stopped and after an announcement in French several passengers exited. We were able to make out a French language message that appeared on a digital display indicating there had been a traffic accident and the train would be delayed for 30 minutes. The times are displayed in military format. Fortunately, we were at a stop close to our destination and exited. If you are on a train and it has been stopped for 5 minutes or longer, you should try to determine the reason and determine an alternate plan such as a taxi, a cafe or a bus at street level, or whether you should wait once you know the approximate restart time. Some local passengers may have no choice as they need the train to get to their final destination and have no feasible alternative.

You can also use Uber in Paris, which some prefer because they accept cards and you know the price upfront. However, it's good to have access to Google on your phone as you may need to use the translator to convey your destination.

Just in case you may lose Internet connection while on the street you could screenshot the destination from your hotel and save your photo to show this to the driver. Please note there are unauthorized taxis operating in Paris as in other major cities, which is why I used the G7 app which summons authorized taxis and shows their progress to your location in real time and automatically charged my credit card so no physical transactions had to occur. Their license tag number is also displayed in the app so you can confirm you are getting into the correct vehicle.

Traffic Turn-Around in front of Arc de Triomphe. Pedestrian walk is under the street (see upper right of photo.) 2023 Preston Brady III

It is said that pickpockets like to operate at stops such as Champs Elysees, Trocader and Louvre. One technique they may use is to stand behind you on the escalators or even on the train. In this case it's good to have a backpack or shoulder bag you can easily shift to the front of you. I used a shoulder bag for excursions as it has several interior zipper line pouches inside the bag and I can shift it from the side of my body to the front when it's crowded. In other words, the items inside the bag could not be picked - they are inside zippered pouches. This maneuver appears to be more difficult or cumbersome if carrying a heavy backpack. Only carry what you need for that day. Who wants to tote around a backpack filled with items that are not going to be needed for a particular excursion? Unburden your backpack before leaving for each journey. It is also said that professional pickpockets are adept at cutting straps, so while during our visit it may not have been as crowded as it will be during the Olympics or during peak seasons, one should also be cognizant of people who may be shoulder to shoulder with you, or pressed up against you from behind. There are also warnings against individuals who may bump into you, as this could be a concerted ploy to distract you even while an accomplice picks your pocket or cuts straps. I have seen advice against using fanny packs, (belt bags, waist bags) probably because wearing one is basically announcing to the world you have valuables inside and only cutting one strap could release the pouch, and one may not notice it due to wearing a belt or other reasons. If you are not carrying a bag then gentlemen should carry their wallet and passport in front pockets. If you are still planning your trip, there are clothing brands especially geared for protecting your personal belongings. While I prefer to wear jeans I do have slacks that have several zipper-protected pockets along the pant legs. One can purchase jeans with additional, protected pockets and this is recommended if you are carrying your passport and money on your person. You are recommended to always have your passport on you. If you are wearing short pants consider those with secure pockets - zippers, snaps or buttons. Except in the fashion district I did not see many local women carrying purses - almost all carried small backpacks or shoulder bags.

If you are an international traveler you basically know what to expect at the airport upon arrival. A few observations: don't necessarily follow the crowd because there are many scenarios for travelers once deboarding a plane. For example other passengers on your flight may be catching another plane, meaning their final destination is not Paris. So don't follow them assuming they are headed to pick up baggage. Also, some of the airport personnel may assume you are trying to enter a boarding gate section of the airport when in fact you are meaning to navigate to the baggage pick-up area - not board another flight. If one of them asks you for your boarding pass then you are in the wrong line. We found some of the airport personnel to be very helpful, very proactive, and even correct misinformation provided by another individual. English was limited in some instances. You will want to navigate to the line designated for your nationality. If you are American, follow the flag symbols to the correct customs gates, or ask personnel who seem to be in abundance to assist with passenger questions. International travelers know there are customs gates for each country, so look for your flag and get in that line. The lines may be long and winding so take an extra look to make sure the line you are in is for the correct customs gate. At one point we were incorrectly directed to the wrong line by an airport helper. Another employee corrected their mistake. It's busy. There are lots of people anxious to get through customs and to their accommodations or connecting flights. All this organized chaos is much bigger than you so just stay calm and go with the flow. Just make sure you are in the right lines.

The customs passport review is automated, meaning you scan your own passport and then enter a small gate booth facing another door. That door will display commands such as step forward or step back. Once the second camera has scanned your face and it matches your passport that you just scanned, the light will turn from red to green and you can exit. There were a few delays in our line in which passenger passports were not being scanned correctly. In one case a passenger finally made it into the gate booth but the second gate would not open. The light remained red. All this caused about a 10 minute delay but finally the passenger made it through the second gate. It is recommended that you hold your passport firmly down on the scanner, instead of just placing it there and expecting it to be correctly scanned. In the case of the passenger who got stuck in the second gate, it appears the scan of her passport was not perfect and although it was enough to open the first gate, the second camera needed more precise information. Hence, press down on your passport during the scan to assure a perfect image capture. One day all of this will be history as everything is moving towards a complete facial recognition process.

You will be showing your passport to a lot of people so either just keep it in your hand or have it conveniently stored for retrieval. Do not leave any bags unattended and this includes sitting bags on the floor several feet from your person. It may appear to personnel or other passengers your bags are unattended and could cause a minor issue. If you are taking a taxi to your accommodations either use the taxi app (G7) or follow the exit (Sortie) signs leading to the exterior taxi stand, which should have an attendant to assist. Of course the French word for exit is sortie so when you are looking to exit the airport or any metro station look for Sortie. The taxi ride from the CDG airport should normally cost about 60 euros, but depending on traffic it could cost a little more, up to 70 or 80 euros., It would be unusual even with heavy traffic for the ride to Paris city center to cost more than 80 euros. There is supposed to be a legislated fixed price for the taxi fare to and from the airport, but I am not sure how strongly it is enforced.

If you want to take a metro train from the airport to the city center, the RER B train runs about every 10 minutes and takes about 30 minutes. During heavy traffic the train option will likely be faster than taking a taxi. If you arrive at the peak or start of the Olympics, traffic will be very heavy so you might plan in advance to navigate to the RER B train which will take you to the metro station Paris Gare du Nord. Depending on where you stay in Paris you may have to transfer to a second train. The 1 RER B train station is near terminal 3 in the Roissypole building. This station is for travelers arriving in terminal 1 and 3. For terminal 2 passengers the train station is between terminal 2E and 2C. Don't hesitate to ask personnel and the question Where is the train station for Paris city center in French is où se trouve la gare pour le centre ville de Paris. All this said, if you are carrying a lot of luggage it's worth the extra money and time to take a taxi.

While my visit to Paris is still fresh in my mind I consider other thoughts and tips that may benefit a first-time traveler to the city. I brought along a small, easy to carry umbrella. Perhaps in November it rains more than in June through August, but when it did rain it was drizzle and sprinkles. We did not experience any downpours. It was very windy at times but that may have been because a large storm had impacted the northern coast. I don't recall seeing umbrellas offered for purchase on a wide scale, although I'm sure they were around somewhere. Another perhaps even more viable option is a rain coat. At home I use a very light Frogg pull-over and it works fine and keeps you hands-free. Also it's easily foldable and will not take up much room in your bag. I wore a pair of water-resistant tennis shoes purchased about 3 weeks prior to arrival so they could be broken in. Fortunately, they fit perfectly and were completely comfortable from the day of purchase. As I navigated the streets of Paris when it was drizzling, my socks and feet remained dry. It goes without saying Paris is a walker's city and *a pair or two of very comfortable shoes is a must*. I also usually wore bluejeans and while these are a little thicker than say polyester or cotton slacks, they also provided protection against the small amount of rain we experienced. In the summer of course travelers may wear shorts or thinner slacks for cooler comfort. In this case a raincoat or umbrella would seem to be a must-have.

To avoid roaming charges for your cell phone usage in and around Paris, check with your phone service provider prior to departure. Some carriers offer an international day pass for a set, daily fee. Roaming can be tricky, and while the more popular restaurants and other establishments offer automatic connection to Wi-Fi, smaller, less popular establishments may not offer Wi-Fi, or you may have to ask. I did not see any establishment post their Wi-Fi password on their menu or anywhere for that matter. Of course most hotels will offer free Wi-Fi and provide the password without having to ask for it. Overall, the Wi-Fi experience was good but there were some glitches, and during the Olympics it is hoped the city of Paris and the rest of France will be prepared for the immense number of users and make arrangements to provide enormous bandwidth with good, fast connections. Most people have no issues using the roaming feature of their phone so they do not have to connect to Wi-Fi, but I recommend confirming you will have this trouble-free option while in Paris, especially if you have more than one phone on your account. I did have an issue while in Paris and was unable to reach my provider by chat or phone. (The chat offered 3 default options none of which applied in my case. Even after I selected any of the 3 options I was directed to "help topics'' which were not helpful.) It was very disappointing and they will be made aware. Having phone issues while on vacation is an unwelcomed distraction. Fortunately, my travel companion, who was using the same service carrier, had no roaming issues and we depended on his phone during times we needed Internet assistance in non-Wi-Fi areas during our trip. There were a few times when we were separated and sent text messages, some of which arrived within seconds, and some that were delayed by minutes or even longer. If you are traveling with others and navigate as a group, it's a good idea to have a plan in case anyone gets separated from the group. For example if the group is taking the train to the Louvre, then it could be agreed that if anyone becomes separated all will meet at the end of the visitor line leading into the museum (the glass pyramid.) If traveling to a restaurant then agree to meet there in the event of separation. Wi-Fi can be spotty so taking screenshots of destinations and translations ahead of time - before you leave for your destination - is very useful because these do not require an Internet connection.

Before leaving the USA we registered for the State Department's STEP program, which should send you alerts and updates should they be needed. We registered for this program and did not receive any alerts during our visit. We did not see any demonstrations, and despite a large number of social media warnings from others, we did not encounter any anti-American incidents or ever felt anyone did not like us because we were Americans. I doubt most people even knew we were Americans because as I wrote earlier, we dressed like normal people in jeans and shirts and tennis shoes just like most of the Parisians and even other tourists we encountered. The only way someone might identify us as Americans is when we spoke English. We felt completely safe, even at night, but we did not stay out past midnight because we are not of the very younger set and had no desire to visit nightclubs or other late night venues, and frankly we were a little worn out from the daily excursions. In any large city as the very early morning hours arrive there are people who have been drinking all night and that can result in unusual encounters and occurrences for people. I recommend caution in that regard, perhaps even an authorized taxi (G7.)

As I stated early in this narrative, it was not meant to be a guidebook or filled with links to web sites and maps. There are already many such publications, and of course with Google and Bing most technical questions are easily solved. I was motivated to write this because I spent several weeks preparing for my own first-time trip to Paris and after I arrived realized how much of the information I found on popular chat boards was not completely accurate, or even timely. Some of the posts I found were from people with screen names - not their own names, and while I understand and respect the need to protect identity for different reasons, I wondered about a few extremely negative reviews that were not authenticated or supported by evidence, and of course the unpleasant odor of trolls sometimes permeated these websites. On the other hand there were numerous posts where it seemed people were genuinely trying to be helpful and informative, and appeared to use their real names. One thing stood out and it really surprised me - a very large number of posts were old - as far back as 5 and 6 years and of course the comments section was long closed. Even with recent posts, search engines still have a difficult time displaying posts in real time - it can take weeks - or much longer - for relevant posts to reach the top-level keyword or key phrase results. By that time you are already in Paris, right? While it was still fresh in my mind, I wanted to write about my trip that occurred from November 1-8th, 2023 and make it available on sites where people would be searching for up-to-date publications. With extra digging I was able to find more recent, even real-time posts about visits to Paris, but it was my own visit, using the techniques I use wherever I travel, that brought continuity and logic to the trip.

I look forward to my next visit to Paris and hope to expand the journey to other regions in France. I realize Paris is not necessarily "France" but on this first trip I did want to immerse myself only in the city. Even though some books and posts indicate you can see Paris in 5 to 7 days, I am here to tell you that barely a dent can be made in that time-frame. The title of my publication might be Seven Days in Paris, but that does not mean I "saw" Paris in seven days. I rubbed elbows with Paris. You may hit upon the major landmarks and several off the beaten path spots, but there is so much more to see, to experience. And for this reason that is why so many people visit Paris time and again. You could take your time and see a lot more if you simply moved there, right? For me Paris was a vacation. It wasn't a business trip, like it will be for many who will be there before, during and after the Olympics. I felt like since I was on vacation I would not find myself rushing from one landmark to the other, to try and squeeze in as much of Paris as possible in 7 days. Do I feel bad about not seeing Versailles? Not really. It's been sitting there for over 400 years and will be there for my next visit.

If you are in Paris mainly for the Olympics you will probably get a good taste of Paris along with your Summer Games activities. During your perhaps short stay in Paris and surrounding areas you will in effect be living there. Plan ahead for the most enjoyable trip possible, but don't over-plan and then expect everything to fall into place. We all know things happen - reservations get lost, equipment stops working, the sun is shining when you have your umbrella and it rains when you don't have it. Your photo app on your phone can turn out to be a very helpful tool. Before you leave, create folders such as Hotel, Restaurants, Museums, Metro, Neighborhoods, Olympic Events. Save electronic tickets to the appropriate folders, that way if there is an issue with connecting to email you will have the documents in a folder that does not require a roaming or Wi-Fi connection. Take a picture of your passport and save it in photos too. Make sure the face ID feature of your phone is the default method of accessing it, or use a password if you prefer. I made two lists using the Notes feature on my phone - a Paris Packing list and a Things to Do Before Leaving for Paris. I checked these lists periodically leading up to my journey, and nothing was left behind and my home was properly prepared for continued sustainability in my absence.

I hope you and yours have a great trip to Paris, and that perhaps I have written something that will prove very helpful to you before and during your stay.

Man walking a dog, Paris 2023, Preston Brady III

About me: I am from, and live with my 7 cats (Betty, Bonnie, Cotton, Angie, Gracie, Spike, Precious, and 3 tortoises Belinda, Betty and Bonnie.)

in Mobile, Alabama where I write fiction and non-fiction full-time. I enjoy herb gardening and blog on my website Herbscapes.com. I enjoy walking in the park, beaches, painting, creating music, and trying to conjure up great culinary dishes. For 14 years beginning in the early Seventies I lived in San Francisco where I attended City College of San Francisco and San Francisco State University majoring in philosophy, and where for 4 years I was a reporter for the quad-lingual newspaper The TenderloinTimes. My first international trip was in the early Eighties to Moscow and Leningrad - now called St. Petersburg, and Helsinki, Finland. Since then I have traveled extensively in Mexico (favorites: San Miguel de Allende and Oaxaca) and have visited Thailand, Japan (twice) – Tokyo!) England, Costa Rica (twice) and many locations throughout the United States. I am author of the satirical novella The Color White, (2022) the story of a Black billionaire who creates a Fifties throwback town in the Deep South and reverses the roles of Blacks and Whites. In 2012 I wrote The Chronicles of Norvovia: Battle of the Bands, set in a fictional Scandinavian country and about a heavy metal battle of the bands competition in which the loser will be exiled from the country. I fully expect both of these novels to be phenomenal bestsellers after I have passed from here to the next journey.

Preston Brady III, Paris, 2023

Made in the USA
Columbia, SC
24 November 2023